*S*ometimes there is a happening in our lives that changes the way we think about ourselves and sends us along a new path. These turning points can come when we are young—through a person we meet, an experience we have, a difficulty we overcome.

Since 1789, only forty-two people have been president of the United States. What has made these forty-two people unique? Was there a turning point in their young lives that caused them to change direction and set them on a path that led them to the White House?

—Judith St. George

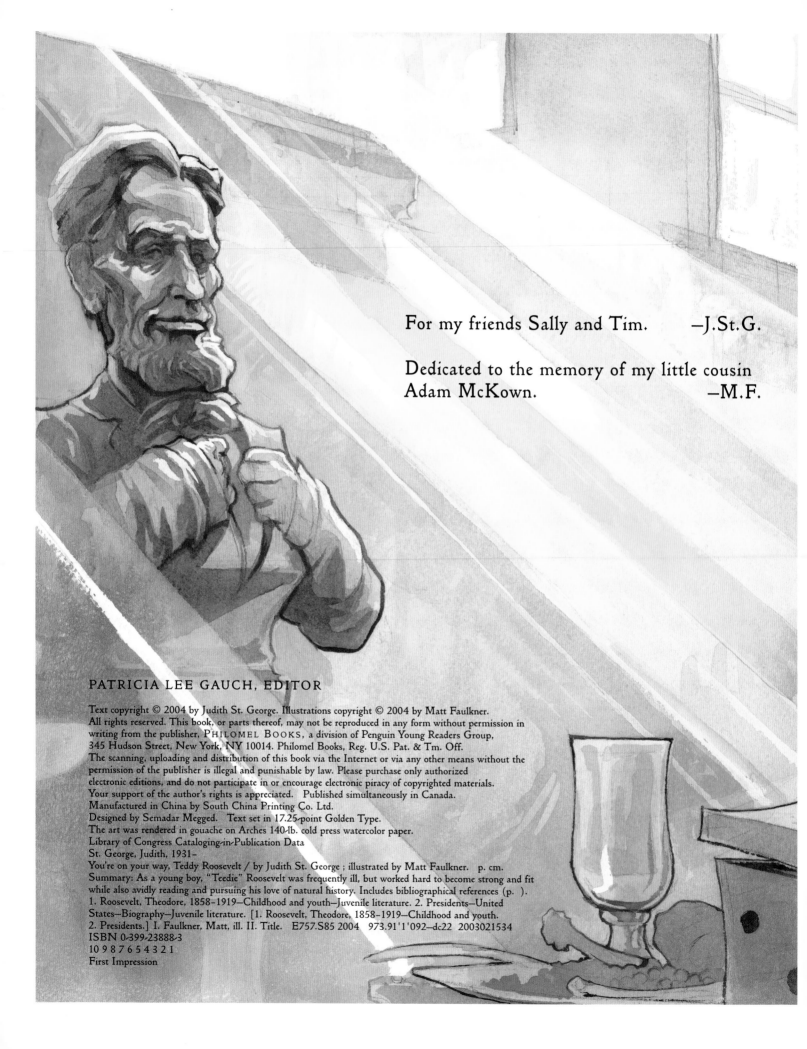

For my friends Sally and Tim. —J.St.G.

Dedicated to the memory of my little cousin
Adam McKown. —M.F.

PATRICIA LEE GAUCH, EDITOR

Text copyright © 2004 by Judith St. George. Illustrations copyright © 2004 by Matt Faulkner.
All rights reserved. This book, or parts thereof, may not be reproduced in any form without permission in
writing from the publisher, PHILOMEL BOOKS, a division of Penguin Young Readers Group,
345 Hudson Street, New York, NY 10014. Philomel Books, Reg. U.S. Pat. & Tm. Off.
The scanning, uploading and distribution of this book via the Internet or via any other means without the
permission of the publisher is illegal and punishable by law. Please purchase only authorized
electronic editions, and do not participate in or encourage electronic piracy of copyrighted materials.
Your support of the author's rights is appreciated.   Published simultaneously in Canada.
Manufactured in China by South China Printing Co. Ltd.
Designed by Semadar Megged.   Text set in 17.25-point Golden Type.
The art was rendered in gouache on Arches 140-lb. cold press watercolor paper.
Library of Congress Cataloging-in-Publication Data
St. George, Judith, 1931–
You're on your way, Teddy Roosevelt / by Judith St. George ; illustrated by Matt Faulkner.   p. cm.
Summary: As a young boy, "Teedie" Roosevelt was frequently ill, but worked hard to become strong and fit
while also avidly reading and pursuing his love of natural history. Includes bibliographical references (p.).
1. Roosevelt, Theodore, 1858–1919—Childhood and youth—Juvenile literature. 2. Presidents—United
States—Biography—Juvenile literature. [1. Roosevelt, Theodore, 1858–1919—Childhood and youth.
2. Presidents.] I. Faulkner, Matt, ill. II. Title.   E757.S85 2004   973.91'1'092—dc22   2003021534
ISBN 0-399-23888-3
10 9 8 7 6 5 4 3 2 1
First Impression

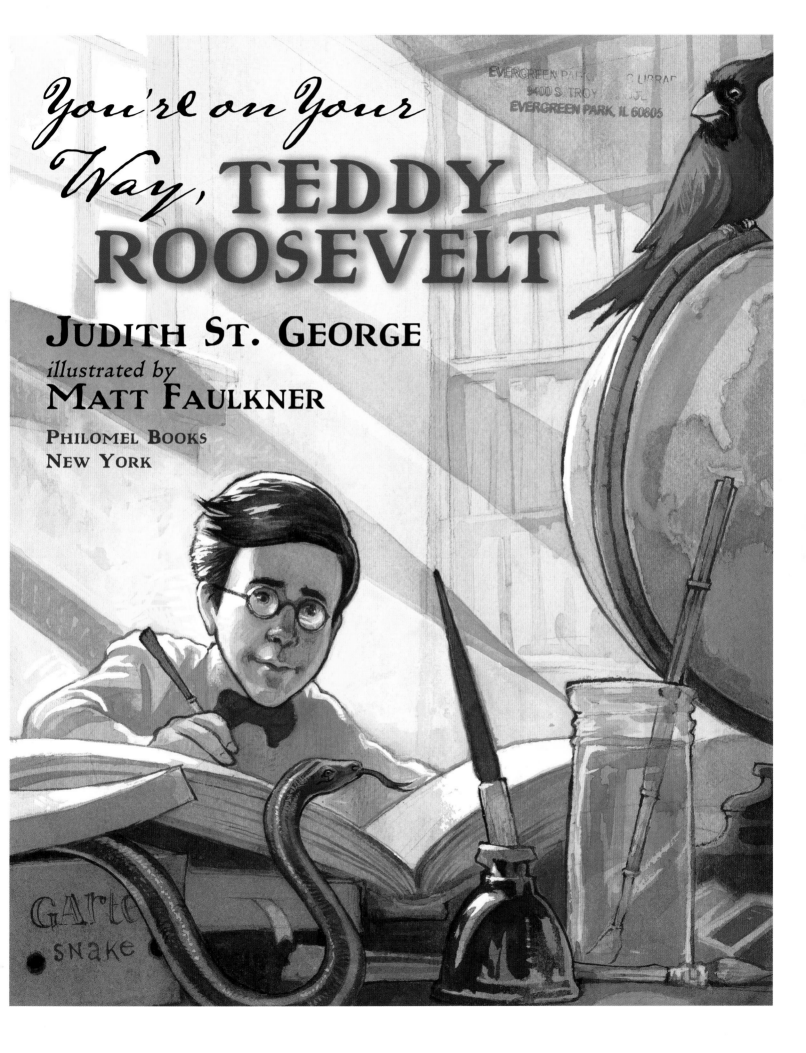

You're on Your
Way, TEDDY
ROOSEVELT

JUDITH ST. GEORGE

illustrated by
MATT FAULKNER

PHILOMEL BOOKS
NEW YORK

Chapter 1. A VERY SMALL PERSON

Teedie sat up in bed. He coughed and wheezed. He couldn't breathe. Papa ran into Teedie's room. Papa always knew what to do. He paced back and forth with Teedie in his arms. At last Teedie could breathe.

Teedie and Papa had the same name—
Theodore Roosevelt. But seven-year-old
Teedie wasn't strong and tall like Papa.
Or handsome.

Teedie was pale and puny.

Grandmamma called him "a very small
person." Teedie coughed and wheezed
with asthma . . . ever since he was three.
He had stomachaches and headaches too.

And nightmares. Sometimes a werewolf crouched at the foot of his bed.

Mama and Papa worried. Whatever would become of their little Teedie? Maybe fresh country air would help his asthma. It was worth a try. Yes, they would go to the country for the summer.

Teedie Roosevelt had always lived with his family in the city—
New York City. New York City was where Teedie had been born on
October 27, 1858.

But New York City was *indoors*. The country was all *outdoors*. Teedie plunged headlong into a new world. Nature! He caught all the "buggies," snakes, salamanders, field mice and turtles he could find. He learned the songs and calls of birds.

Teedie, his younger brother Elliott—called Ellie—and his younger sister Corinne—called Conie—became We 3. Teedie was their ringleader. We 3 ran barefoot, played Indians, built wigwams, climbed trees and rode their pony named General Grant.

The country air did help Teedie's asthma. A little. But even in the country Teedie got sick. Teedie, in bed, was still We 3's ringleader. He told made-up, to-be-continued stories to Ellie and Conie. Teedie's hero? A small boy (like himself) who talked with the animals.

One day, after their return to New York City, Teedie saw the body of a seal outside a market. Why, New York was *outdoors* too. Teedie measured the seal from head to toe. He had a hundred questions. What had the seal's life been like? Where had it been? How had it gotten into the city's harbor?

When the seal was taken away, Teedie was given the skull. Hurrah! He would start his very own museum.

The Roosevelt Museum of Natural History was in Teedie's bedroom at 28 East Twentieth Street. Teedie filled his museum with small creatures (both dead *and* alive). But not everyone was happy.

The upstairs maid refused to enter his room. The washerwoman wouldn't do the laundry with a snapping turtle tied to the sink. Guests checked their water pitchers for snakes.

Once Teedie took off his hat on a city streetcar. Frogs that were perched on his head leapt to the streetcar floor. Mama even threw a litter of dead mice out of the icebox.

"Oh, the loss to science," Teedie moaned.
"Oh, the loss."

Good times for Teedie were finding small creatures for his museum. Adventures with We 3 were good times too. But bad times, when he coughed and wheezed with asthma, still lurked in the shadows.

Chapter 2. MAKE YOUR BODY!

Teedie was ten when Mama and Papa told the family they were all going to Europe . . . for a year. Mama and Papa again had high hopes. The ocean voyage and the change of scene were sure to be good for Teedie.

But Teedie had never heard such terrible news. A year with no hunting for birds' nests. Or catching frogs and "buggies." At least We 3 and their older sister, Anna, known as Bamie, wouldn't miss school. They didn't go to school. Their aunt Anna was their teacher. Right in their New York City brownstone house.

Grandpappa Roosevelt had high hopes for Teedie's health too. He wrote Teedie a poem.

We all shall gladly see you back
Again at your home
And hope that sickness may no more
Compel your feet to roam.

In May 1869 the Roosevelts and all their trunks bounced over New York's cobblestone streets to the pier. Teedie cried almost the whole way. He already missed his museum.

ROMA

Paris

DEUTSCH

e great fun.
ma and We three
had a fine row on
the river then took
a stroll on a fat
pony!
Very affection-
-ately, Teedie

Grand Papa Roosevelt
Union Square
New York City, N.Y.
U.S.A.

In Europe, Teedie fought asthma, headaches, stomachaches *and* nightmares in sixty-six different hotels. He hadn't wanted to come. He didn't want to be here. Now when he was sick, he wasn't even in his own bed.

When Teedie coughed and wheezed, Papa held Teedie in his arms and paced. Or gentle Mama stroked his forehead and told stories of her southern childhood.

He saw doctors in almost every country. Sometimes Mama or Papa—usually Papa—rushed him to a country lodge or seaside inn for a change of air. Papa even gave Teedie coffee to drink and cigars to smoke to help his breathing.

But when Teedie wasn't sick, he climbed mountains, hiked and toured museums, castles, churches and zoos. He *said* he hated the whole year. But he wrote in his diary: "Fine fun . . . a jolly walk . . . a happy day!"

In May 1870 the Roosevelts and all their trunks bounced back to 28 East Twentieth Street. (Bamie stayed behind in a French school.)

"New York!!! Hip! Hurrah!" Teedie cheered in his diary.

Teedie had taken an ocean voyage. He'd had a change of scene. He had breathed country air. But his asthma wasn't one bit better.

Off he went to a famous New York doctor. Teedie's lungs were crowded into his narrow chest, and asthma still crowded his lungs, the famous doctor told Mama and Papa. Teedie should have "plenty of fresh air," plus exercise to expand his lungs.

Papa sat Teedie down and looked him right in the eye. "Theodore, you have the mind, but not the body," he said. "You must *make* your body. It is hard drudgery to make one's body, but I know you will do it."

Papa was Teedie's hero. If only he could be like Papa, strong and tall. Teedie set his jaw and clenched his teeth. "I'll make my body," he promised his father. And he would.

Chapter 3. THE GYM

By now Teedie was a big reader. Soon after his talk with Papa, Teedie read a poem. Part of the poem read:

> . . . the pertest little ape
> That ever affronted human shape,
> . . . all legs and length,
> With blood for bone, all speed, no strength.

That was him. All speed, no strength. There was no time to lose. He had to start exercising. Now! Papa took charge. He signed Teedie up at John Wood's Gymnasium.

The gymnasium smelled of liniment and sweat. But it was no hole-in-the-wall. Mama and Papa called the New Yorkers who exercised there "people of good family" . . . just like the Roosevelts.

When Teedie went to the gym, Mama went too. Mama was small and beautiful. She liked to wear fine dresses, and hats, and gloves.

Did she look out of place in the gym? Yes. (She didn't care.)
Teedie worked out on the weight machines. He pulled the weights up, let them ride down, then pulled them up again. It looked boring. But Teedie didn't find anything boring that expanded his chest and built up his puny body.

How about having a gym right in their own house? Then Teedie could exercise any time he wanted. That was Mama's idea.

Papa took charge . . . as usual. He had a second-floor wall knocked down to make space. Then he hired John Wood to bring in weights, parallel bars, a leather pommel horse, a chinning bar, a punching bag and dumbbells.

Teedie worked out every day—when he was well.

In 1871 the Roosevelts traveled to Long Island for the summer. Teedie was still sick from time to time. But his exercise and workouts paid off. He had grown stronger. He swam, rowed, ran races, rode horseback and held tree-climbing contests with Ellie and cousins of all ages—when he was well. Sick or well, Teedie read books by the dozens.

In August, Papa treated the family to a monthlong camping trip in the Adirondack Mountains. Roosevelts being Roosevelts, uncles, aunts and cousins came along. And Papa decided Teedie could go too.

What an adventure! Teedie hiked in the woods, climbed mountains, fished, shot rapids and slept under the stars. Camping was everything that he'd hoped it would be. He was hooked on the camping life forever.

In Europe, Teedie hadn't gone more than a few days without falling sick. In the Adirondack Mountains, he went a whole month without one single asthma attack.

Chapter 4. **A MIRACLE!**

Teedie liked birds and small animals around him . . . whether they were alive or not. And he wanted to learn all about them close-up. After all, he was a scientist. When Teedie was thirteen, he learned how to skin, stuff and mount small creatures.

Teedie had never been neat. Now he was messier than ever. His brother, Ellie, wrote:

> There was an old fellow named Teedie,
> Whose clothes at best looked so seedy
> That his friends in dismay
> Hollered out, "Oh, I say!"
> At this dirty old fellow named Teedie.

Ellie's teasing didn't bother Teedie. But he *was* bothered when he ran out of animals and birds to study.

Papa took charge . . . as usual. He gave Teedie a double-barreled shotgun. Though Teedie blazed away, he never hit anything. When his cousins took a turn, they shot at birds and animals that Teedie couldn't even see. One day Teedie's friends pointed out a billboard. Teedie could make out the billboard, but not the message. How puzzling!

Papa was in charge . . . again. He took Teedie to an eye doctor. At thirteen, Teedie read more than ever. He could see close-up to read, but everything far away was a blur. Teedie was nearsighted.

Teedie was fitted with glasses. City street signs, a distant horse and carriage and clouds overhead jumped into focus.

So that was why he tripped over things. He wasn't clumsy. He hadn't been able to see where he was going. What else had he missed?

He had missed spotting birds, that's what. Teedie had extra-good hearing. He always described birds by their songs and calls: "wheezy notes . . . trills . . . chirps." Now he could name birds by sight. His new glasses were a miracle.

Chapter 5. THE WEAKLING

Teedie's new glasses changed his life. Maybe his health would change for the better too. But just before Teedie turned fourteen, he coughed and wheezed with one of his worst asthma attacks ever.

Mama and Papa agreed something had to be done. What about sending Teedie to Maine, where the air was clear and cool?

Teedie traveled alone to Maine. Two boys about Teedie's age on the stagecoach spotted Teedie's thick glasses, big teeth and skinny wrists sticking out of his city suit. A perfect victim. The boys began to tease.

Teedie had never faced bullies before. Or played rough games on a school playground.

He tried to ignore the teasing. That didn't help. At last he couldn't take any more. He lunged at the two boys. But the boys quickly pinned him down.

Teedie was crushed. He had always dreamed of being like true-life heroes: "Men who were fearless and could hold their own in the world." But look at him. Two years of bodybuilding and he was still a first-class weakling.

Teedie had to learn to give as good as he got.
How about boxing lessons? That ought to do it.

When Teedie returned home from Maine, Papa and Mama gave their approval. As always, Papa went for the best. He hired an ex-prizefighter to be Teedie's boxing master.

With clenched teeth and set jaw, Teedie began. But his eyes, brain and feet didn't seem to work together. He had to admit that he was "a painfully slow and awkward pupil."

Slow or not, Teedie began to improve. He was as skinny as ever. But now he put some muscle into his punches. He learned to duck and dodge. And then one day he won a first-place pewter mug in a lightweight boxing match. What a victory!

He'd come a long way since those boys on the stagecoach had pinned him down. Just let some bully try teasing him now.

Chapter 6. A BATTLE WON

Teedie didn't get the chance to take on bullies. In October 1872 the family went on another yearlong trip. The best stopover? Egypt. For two months the Roosevelts cruised up the Nile River in their very own boat.

The Nile Valley was filled with birds that Teedie had never seen or even read about. He mounted more than a hundred birds and labeled them in Latin for his museum. They would always remind him of his sun-filled days in Egypt.

The Roosevelts arrived back in New York in November 1873. But home was no longer 28 East Twentieth Street.

Home was now 6 West Fifty-seventh Street, a new, built-to-order mansion with a ballroom, a billiard room and a top-floor gymnasium. Teedie's museum was tucked away in the attic.

For the next two years Teedie worked with a tutor. Harvard College was his goal. He studied German, French, Greek, Latin, English, math, science, geography and history.

In his free time—he didn't have much—he boxed, wrestled, skated in Central Park and worked out. In the summer he rode horseback, swam and rowed.

Teedie was still stick-thin, but his sports and workouts had built up his body.

Almost-seventeen-year-old Teedie proudly listed his measurements:
Chest—34 inches; Waist—26 1/2 inches; Weight—124 pounds;
Height—5 feet 8 inches.

The time had come to show the world how far he'd come. A
field day, that would do it. In August 1875 Teedie, Ellie
and their cousins put their heads together at the
Roosevelts' Long Island estate. They came up
with fifteen different sporting events.

The Big Day came and the competition was fierce. Each boy (especially Teedie) was out to win. They high-jumped, pole-vaulted, ran, long-jumped, wrestled and boxed.

The big-time winner? Teedie! Out of fifteen events, he won fourteen. Would this have been possible even three years ago? Never. That showed everyone how far he'd come, all right.

By his own strong will, Teedie had at last won the battle for his body. It wasn't as if he never coughed and wheezed with asthma or fell sick again, because he did. And he wasn't a muscle-bound star athlete either.

But from his first workout in Wood's Gymnasium he had been determined to control his asthma and illnesses rather than letting his asthma and illnesses control him. And he had. On that hot summer day in August he had proved to himself—and everyone else—that he had taken charge of his own life.

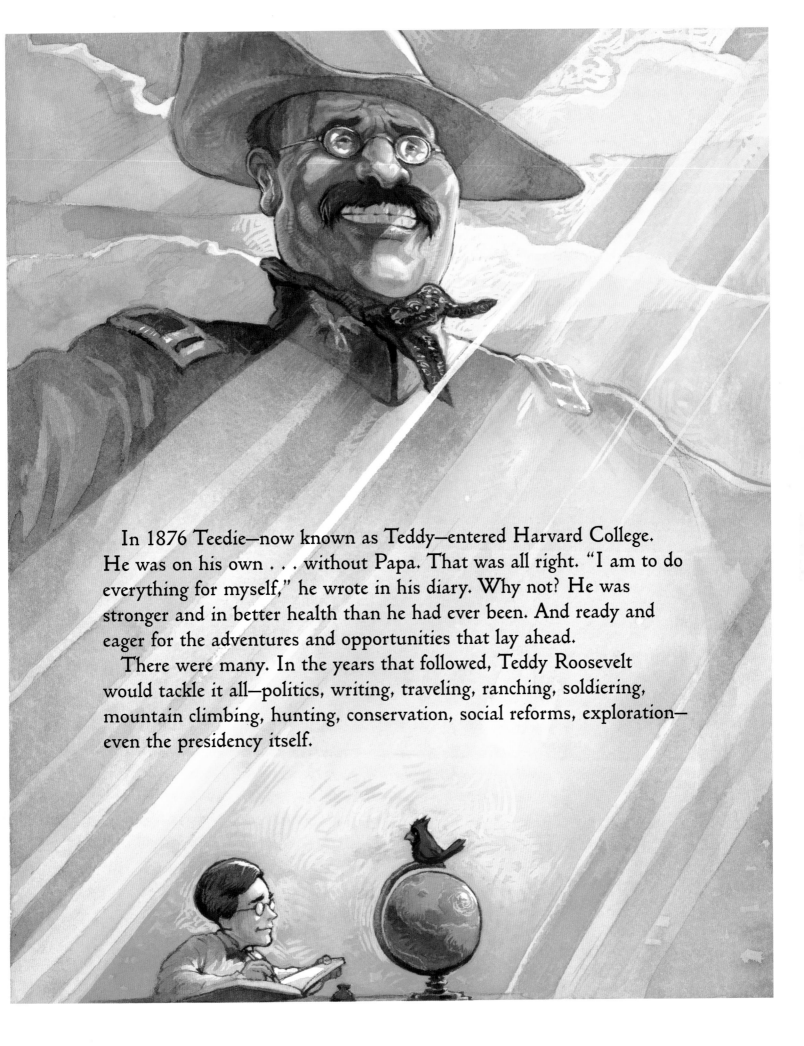

In 1876 Teedie—now known as Teddy—entered Harvard College. He was on his own . . . without Papa. That was all right. "I am to do everything for myself," he wrote in his diary. Why not? He was stronger and in better health than he had ever been. And ready and eager for the adventures and opportunities that lay ahead.

There were many. In the years that followed, Teddy Roosevelt would tackle it all—politics, writing, traveling, ranching, soldiering, mountain climbing, hunting, conservation, social reforms, exploration— even the presidency itself.

Theodore Roosevelt was born into a wealthy New York City family on October 27, 1858. Teedie, as he was known, was a bright boy who was tutored at home by governesses. Throughout his childhood, Teedie was plagued by asthma and other illnesses. Determined to improve his health, he exercised faithfully in a gymnasium set up in the Roosevelt home.

After graduating from Harvard, Roosevelt was elected to the New York State Assembly. He went on to serve as president of the New York City Board of Police Commissioners, and was elected governor of New York State in 1898. He also pursued the "strenuous life" as a rancher, naturalist, explorer, author and colonel of the Rough Riders during the Spanish-American War.

Republican Vice President Theodore Roosevelt became the twenty-sixth president of the United States in 1901 when President William McKinley was assassinated. As president, Roosevelt steered reform bills through Congress that regulated big business, protected Americans from unsafe foods, set aside millions of acres of land for public use and expanded the U.S. Navy. Roosevelt also engineered the building of the Panama Canal and settled a war between Russia and Japan, which won him the Nobel Peace Prize.

In 1904 Theodore Roosevelt was elected to the presidency in his own right. As a reform president, he improved millions of American lives and worked for greater democracy for all citizens. Abroad he expanded America's role as a world power. He brought new vigor and strength to the presidency by his dynamic leadership.

Much of Theodore Roosevelt's retirement was spent enjoying the strenuous life he loved, hunting in Africa and exploring the Amazon River. He died in January 1919 at the age of 60.

BIBLIOGRAPHY

Fritz, Jean. *Bully for You, Teddy Roosevelt!* New York: G. P. Putnam's, 1991.

Garraty, John A. *Theodore Roosevelt: The Strenuous Life.* New York: American Heritage Publishing Co., 1967.

McCullough, David. *Mornings on Horseback.* New York: Simon & Schuster, 1981.

Miller, Nathan. *Theodore Roosevelt: A Life.* New York: William Morrow and Company, Inc., 1992.

Morison, Elting. *The Letters of Theodore Roosevelt: 1868-1898.* Vol. I. Cambridge, Mass.: Harvard University Press, 1951.

Morris, Edmund. *The Rise of Theodore Roosevelt.* New York: Coward, McCann & Geoghegan, Inc., 1979.

Putnam, Carleton. *Theodore Roosevelt: The Formative Years, 1858-1886.* Vol. I. New York: Charles Scribner's Sons, 1958.

Roosevelt, Theodore. *Theodore Roosevelt: An Autobiography.* New York: The Macmillan Company, 1913.

Roosevelt, Theodore. *Theodore Roosevelt's Diaries of Boyhood and Youth.* New York: Charles Scribner's Sons, 1928.